ZODIAC SIGNS

# AQUARIUS

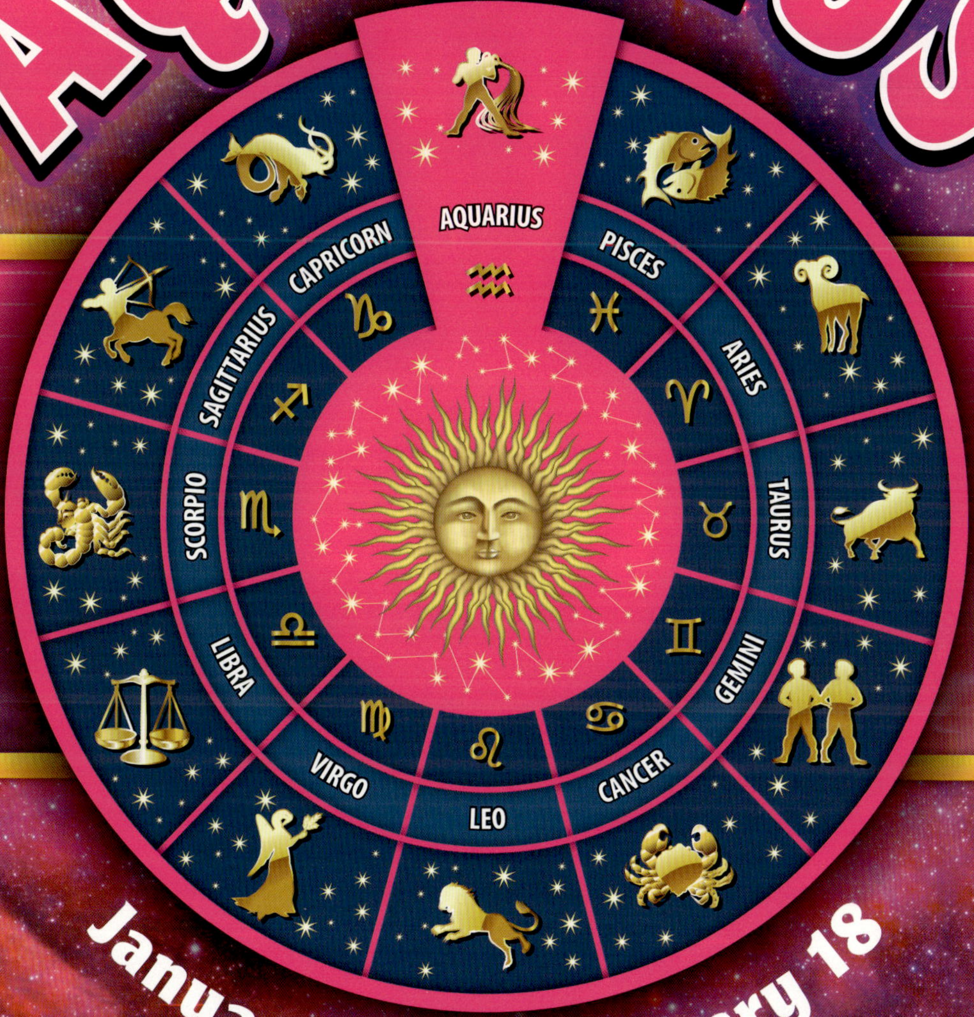


## January 20 - February 18

Linda Hopkins

AV2
www.av2books.com

Step 1
Go to **www.av2books.com**

Step 2
Enter this unique code

**IBAXWOK5P**

Step 3
Explore your interactive eBook!

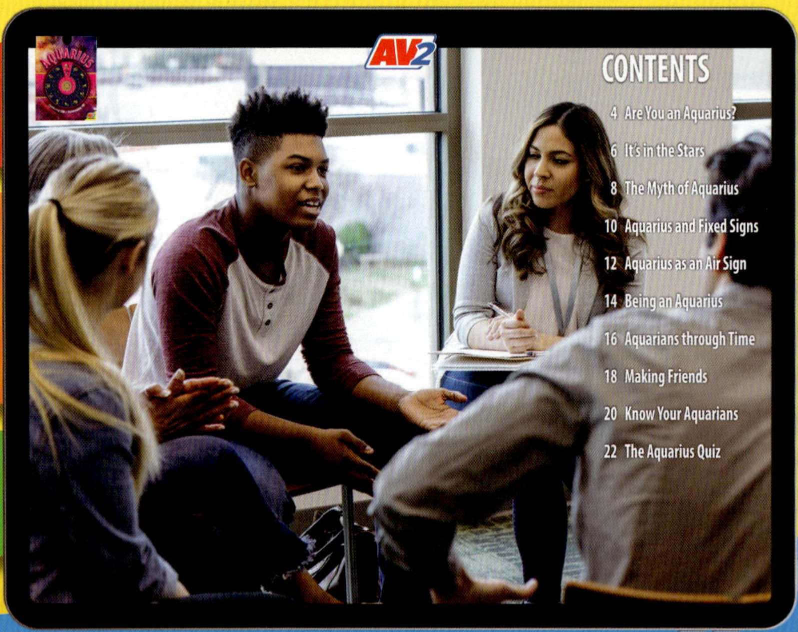


**AV2 is optimized for use on any device**

# Your interactive eBook comes with...

**Contents**
Browse a live contents page to easily navigate through resources

**Audio**
Listen to sections of the book read aloud

**Videos**
Watch informative video clips

**Weblinks**
Gain additional information for research

**Try This!**
Complete activities and hands-on experiments

**Key Words**
Study vocabulary, and complete a matching word activity

**Quizzes**
Test your knowledge

**Slideshows**
View images and captions

**... and much, much more!**

ZODIAC SIGNS

# AQUARIUS

**January 20 – February 18**

## Contents

# Are You an Aquarius?

Do you spend much of your time thinking? Are you someone who comes up with ideas and solutions? If this sounds familiar, you might be an Aquarius. An Aquarius is someone who was born between January 20 and February 18.

Aquarius is a sign in the zodiac. The zodiac is a series of 12 **constellations** that run across the night sky. For centuries, people have used these groups of stars to tell the future. The study of the stars in this manner is called astrology.

# Zodiac Chart

**A person's zodiac sign is determined by his or her date of birth. Which sign matches your birthday?**

# It's in the Stars

The zodiac constellations form a circle around Earth. In one year, Earth makes a full **orbit** around the Sun. As it does this, the Sun appears to be in different places at set times. The zodiac constellations are found along the path the Sun appears to follow.

Long ago, people used the Sun to tell the time of year. In late January, the Sun passed through the Aquarius constellation. People born then were said to be born under the sign of Aquarius.

Over time, the position of the constellations shifted. Even though the Sun now passes through Aquarius at a different time, the dates associated with the sign of Aquarius remain the same.

**Aquarius's brightest star** is a yellow supergiant called **Beta Aquarii**.

Another star in **Aquarius**, **EZ Aquarii**, is the **12th-closest** star to Earth.

*Aquarius* is Latin for "cup bearer" or "water bearer." It is one of the oldest constellations.

# The Myth of Aquarius

The ancient Greeks had stories about how each zodiac constellation came to be in the sky. Aquarius is linked to Ganymede, the cup bearer to the gods.

One day, a handsome prince named Ganymede was out herding sheep. Zeus, the father of men and gods, saw Ganymede on the hillside. He was struck by Ganymede's good looks.

Zeus turned himself into an eagle and caught Ganymede in his talons. Zeus then flew Ganymede to Olympus, the home of the gods, so he could serve as their cup bearer. Zeus also made Ganymede **immortal** and gave him eternal youth.

Ganymede lives on to this day in the night sky. The image of the cup bearer can still be seen as the constellation Aquarius.

Ganymede was the son of King Tros, ruler of Troy.

# Aquarius and Fixed Signs

In astrology, some zodiac signs share certain **qualities**. These qualities show how a person acts in the world. The qualities are separated into three groups. Cardinal signs are known for coming up with ideas. Fixed signs ensure things are done properly. Mutable signs adapt when plans suddenly change.

Aquarius is a fixed sign. People in this group are very committed to seeing things through. They are steady and stable, and work steadily toward their goals. Fixed signs are often great achievers as well.

✶ Fixed signs are happiest when they have a project on which to focus their attention.

# Zodiac Signs
## by Quality

### Cardinal Signs
Are known for coming up with ideas.

Aries | Cancer | Libra | Capricorn

### Fixed Signs
Ensure things are done properly.

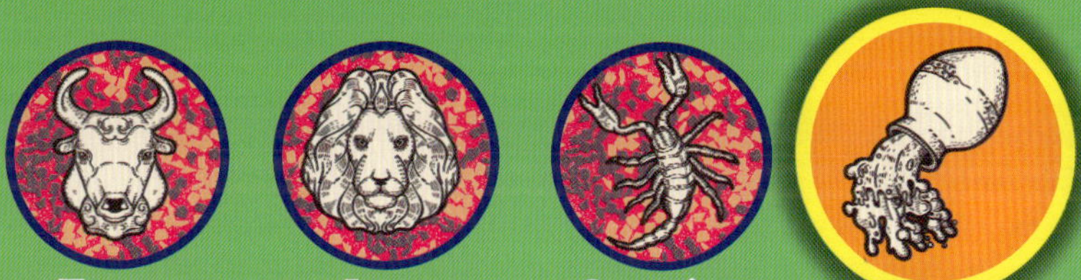

Taurus | Leo | Scorpio | Aquarius

### Mutable Signs
Adapt when plans suddenly change.

Gemini | Virgo | Sagittarius | Pisces

# Aquarius as an Air Sign

Zodiac signs are also grouped according to the four **classical elements**. These are fire, earth, water, and air. Signs that belong to the same group share common personality traits.

Aquarius is an air sign. Air people are deep thinkers. They use **intellect** and reason to work through issues. Air people can see how the work they do may help others and the world. They are also very good at communicating with other people.

Air signs are known for being extremely intelligent.

# Zodiac Signs
## by Element

# Being an Aquarius

An Aquarius's air traits and fixed qualities combine to create a specific type of person. A key Aquarius strength is the ability to solve problems. Aquarians work well on their own, but they enjoy helping others. They see a world full of possibilities.

Aquarians have their weaknesses as well. They can be impatient with people who do not understand their ideas. This may make them seem distant or unfriendly. Aquarians can also get bored easily. Sometimes, they may need to escape from others.

There have been **five U.S. presidents born under Aquarius**. Along with Scorpio, this is the **most** of any zodiac sign.

Today, **Aquarius is ruled by Uranus**, one of the **coldest** planets. Uranus takes **84 Earth years** to orbit around the Sun **once**.

Aquarians are always willing to assist someone in need.

# Aquarians through Time

Aquarians have had a significant impact on the world over time. They have studied the stars, led nations, and brought attention to social **injustices**. Their contributions have helped make the world what it is today.

**1609**

**Astronomer** and mathematician **Galileo Galilei** (born February 15, 1564) creates a powerful **telescope** that allows him to track the phases of the Moon and see stars that cannot be seen with the naked eye.

Author **Charles Dickens** (born February 7, 1812) writes *A Christmas Carol* in only a few weeks.

**1843**

Inventor **Thomas Edison** (born February 11, 1847) perfects the electric light bulb.

**1879**

**1955**

Activist **Rosa Parks** (born February 4, 1913) makes history when she refuses to give up her bus seat to a white man.

**1861**

Lawyer **Abraham Lincoln** (born February 12, 1809) becomes the 16th president of the United States.

**2019**

Actor **Mahershala Ali** (born February 16, 1974) becomes the second African American man to win more than one Oscar for acting, and the first to win two Oscars for Best Supporting Actor.

# Making Friends

Some people believe that zodiac signs can help people form relationships. Each sign has its own traits. These traits can be a good fit with other signs. An Aquarius can use zodiac signs to help decide if someone might be a good friend.

## It's Friendship

**Aquarians get along well with people born under these signs.**

Sagittarius

Gemini

Aries

# It's Love

Aquarians often find romance with these signs.

Aries

Gemini

Libra

# It's Complicated

Aquarians find it difficult to form bonds with these signs.

Pisces

Taurus

Capricorn

# Know Your Aquarians

Aquarians continue to make an impact on the world. They can be found doing good work in various fields. Did you know these people are Aquarians?

## Harry Styles

**Born:** February 1, 1994

Singer Harry Styles first became famous as a member of the band, One Direction. In 2017, he released his first solo single, "Sign of the Times." Harry has also branched out into acting. He played a role in the critically acclaimed film *Dunkirk*.

Harry was nominated for two Teen Choice Awards for his performance in *Dunkirk*.

## Jennifer Aniston

**Born:** February 11, 1969

Actress Jennifer Aniston first rose to fame as Rachel Green on the television show *Friends*. She won an Emmy and a Golden Globe Award for the role. Since 2019, Jennifer has starred in *The Morning Show*. She won a Screen Actors Guild (SAG) Award for her performance in 2020.

## Michael Jordan

**Born:** February 17, 1963

Athlete Michael Jordan is widely considered to be the greatest basketball player in the history of the National Basketball Association (NBA). He was named the NBA's Most Valuable Player (MVP) of the Year five times. In 2016, he was awarded the Presidential Medal of Freedom, the country's highest **civilian** honor.

## Oprah Winfrey

**Born:** January 29, 1954

Oprah Winfrey achieved fame as the host of *The Oprah Winfrey Show*, which lasted 25 seasons. In addition to her film and television credits, Oprah started her own television production company, film production company, and magazine. She also supports charities around the world.

## Ed Sheeran

**Born:** February 17, 1991

Ed Sheeran was born in northern England. He launched his singing career by moving to London when he was only a teenager. In 2015, he won two Grammy Awards for the song "Thinking Out Loud." In 2017, he won two more Grammys, one for the album *Divide* and one for the song "Shape of You."

# The Aquarius QUIZ

**1** Why do people study astrology?

**2** What is the name of Aquarius's brightest star?

**3** What role did Ganymede play to the gods?

**4** To which elemental group does Aquarius belong?

**5** What is a key Aquarius strength?

**6** Which Aquarian perfected the electric light bulb?

**7** Which zodiac signs make good friends for Aquarians?

**8** Which Aquarian athlete was awarded the Presidential Medal of Freedom?

ANSWERS: 1. To tell the future 2. Beta Aquarii 3. Cup bearer 4. Air 5. Problem solving 6. Thomas Edison 7. Sagittarius, Aries, and Gemini 8. Michael Jordan

# Key Words

**astronomer:** a person who studies the science of the Sun, Moon, stars, planets, and other heavenly bodies

**civilian:** a person not belonging to the police force or armed services

**classical elements:** materials from which all other materials were once believed to be made

**constellations:** groups of stars that form patterns in the sky

**immortal:** able to live forever

**injustices:** unfair acts or occurrences

**intellect:** the ability to understand and to think in an intelligent way

**orbit:** a regular, repeating path that one object in space takes around another

**qualities:** traits that make something what it is

**telescope:** an instrument that makes distant objects appear nearer

# Index

Published by AV2
14 Penn Plaza 9th Floor
New York, NY 10122
Website: www.av2books.com





Library of Congress Control Number: 2020938530

ISBN 978-1-7911-2606-3 (hardcover)
ISBN 978-1-7911-2607-0 (softcover)
ISBN 978-1-7911-2608-7 (multi-user eBook)
ISBN 978-1-7911-2609-4 (single-user eBook)

Printed in Guangzhou, China
1 2 3 4 5 6 7 8 9 0 24 23 22 21 20

062020
101119

Editor: Katie Gillespie
Art Director: Terry Paulhus

Every reasonable effort has been made to trace ownership and to obtain permission to reprint copyright material. The publisher would be pleased to have any errors or omissions brought to their attention so that they may be corrected in subsequent printings.

AV2 acknowledges Getty Images, Alamy, iStock, and Shutterstock as its primary image suppliers for this title.